The FIRESIDE BOOK

**A picture and a poem
for every mood
chosen by**

DAVID HOPE

Printed and Published by
D.C. THOMSON & CO., LTD.
185 Fleet Street, London EC4A 2HS.

DREAM-PEDLARY

IF there were dreams to sell,
  What would you buy?
Some cost a passing bell;
  Some a light sigh,
That shakes from Life's fresh crown
Only a rose-leaf down.
If there were dreams to sell,
Merry and sad to tell,
And the crier rang the bell,
  What would you buy?

A cottage lone and still,
  With bowers nigh,
Shadowy, my woes to still,
  Until I die.
Such pearl from Life's fresh crown
Fain would I shake me down,
Were dreams to have at will,
This would best heal my ill,
  This would I buy.

Thomas Lovell Beddoes

THE MARKET SQUARE

YOU know, it hasn't changed at all;
    The church is there—each mould'ring wall
Still beautiful; the silvered stones
Still brood above the churchyard's bones,
The tall old houses reach up high
As if they seek to touch the sky.

Inns there are to offer cheer—
The Bell, The Crown, and others near,
To serve the farmers on their way
To bid for stock on market day,
And housewives buying from the stalls,
New linen, china, tops and balls.

The shops are shaded—cafes, too,
Sun-canopied in pink and blue.
The horse-trough glistens in the sun,
And though the horse's day is done,
There's still a dog that likes a drink
From that old stone-built lichened sink.

Time stands still as the shadows fall
Down from the roofs and chimneys tall
On to the cobbles on the square,
Over the pigeons strutting there.
Then, from the steepness of the tower,
The church clock chimes the tea-time hour.

Violet Hall

TO MIRANDA IN A DONKEY-CART

ALONG the winding, flowery lanes,
   Threading the empty, sunlit land,
A small brown donkey and a shabby cart
   Creep to the sea and the untrodden sand.
A lark mounts up, high as the day is long,
And you beside me make another song.

You sing of waves and whales and hidden caves,
   Of mermaid palaces and starry night;
The world's an ocean where you dip your net
   To fish up gleaming treasures of delight.
The lark shakes out his notes, then folds a wing
And sudden drops to earth. But still you sing.

Yours are winged thoughts. The donkey, what are
   his?
   Do dreams as old as Egypt fill his brain?
Where now Welsh foxgloves chime does he behold
   A fig tree leaning in a dusty plain?
I have no thoughts, but wishes. Would that we
For ever might go ambling to the sea.

Eiluned Lewis

HEAD-GEAR

MR BENSON'S bowler means
   The 8.15 for town.
It complements his city suit,
   His grave, portentious frown,
His briefcase and his leather gloves,
   His scarf and walking-stick,
And as he hurries down the street
   His step is firm and quick.

But Mr Benson's Panama
   Portrays an easier mind.
The city's shadows melt away
   And care is left behind.
He'll get his shears and mower out
   Intending (it would seem)
To work; then, leaning on his fence
   He'll smoke his pipe—and dream.

Gertrude Monro-Higgs

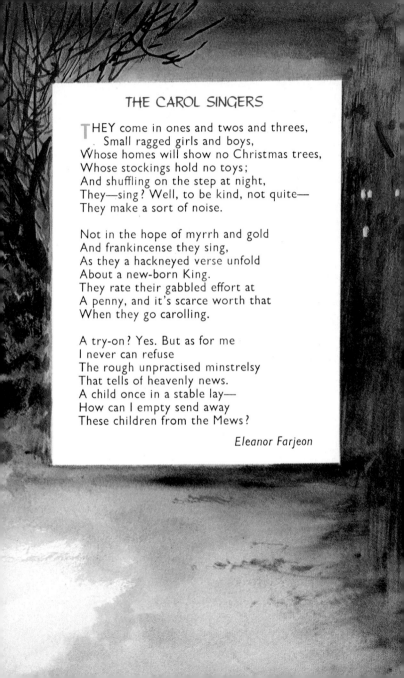

THE CAROL SINGERS

THEY come in ones and twos and threes,
  Small ragged girls and boys,
Whose homes will show no Christmas trees,
Whose stockings hold no toys;
And shuffling on the step at night,
They—sing? Well, to be kind, not quite—
They make a sort of noise.

Not in the hope of myrrh and gold
And frankincense they sing,
As they a hackneyed verse unfold
About a new-born King.
They rate their gabbled effort at
A penny, and it's scarce worth that
When they go carolling.

A try-on? Yes. But as for me
I never can refuse
The rough unpractised minstrelsy
That tells of heavenly news.
A child once in a stable lay—
How can I empty send away
These children from the Mews?

Eleanor Farjeon

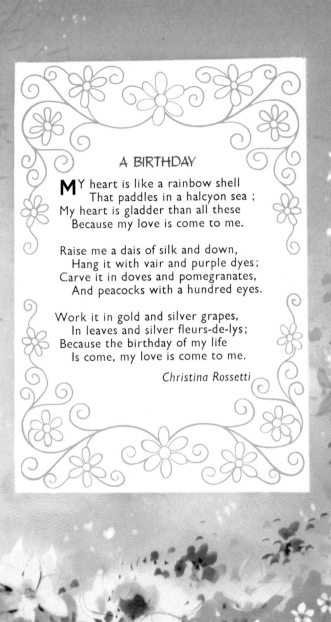

A BIRTHDAY

MY heart is like a rainbow shell
    That paddles in a halcyon sea ;
My heart is gladder than all these
    Because my love is come to me.

Raise me a dais of silk and down,
    Hang it with vair and purple dyes;
Carve it in doves and pomegranates,
    And peacocks with a hundred eyes.

Work it in gold and silver grapes,
    In leaves and silver fleurs-de-lys;
Because the birthday of my life
    Is come, my love is come to me.

Christina Rossetti

400 YEARS AGO

IF I had been a Spaniard in the stirring days of old,
    When Spain had conquered Mexico and searched this
       land for gold,
And you had been an Indian maid (you could have been, you
       know)
We might have met at Benque, at ancient Indian Benque,
We might have met at Benque in the days of long ago.

With armour dull and dented from the dew and rain and
       blows,
I might have ridden up the paths near where the river flows;
You might have gone to worship at the temple on the hill,
And perchance I might have seen you, strolling homewards
       into Benque;
And we might have met near Benque, in the evening calm and
       still.

Like Montezuma's daughter fair, you might have glanced aside,
And wondered at the stranger on his horse's back astride,
I might have seen you enter in your father's dwelling place,
And at night I might have lingered, as the moonlight played on
       Benque,
Yes, I might have stayed in Benque just to gaze upon your face.

It's all changed now at Benque, and the world has altered, too,
But the river and the hills remain, as such things always do;
And I went there and I saw it all, and now I dream — just so —
Of what might have chanced at Benque — in the old days of
       the Spaniards —
Had we met our fate at Benque in the days of long ago.

D. J. Verity

TO BUNTY'S SATCHEL

WELL, yes! Of honest wear and tear
　　You've shouldered manfully your share.
And you have suffered many things
Without complaints or murmurings.

Bulging with books and pencil box,
You have had bangs and sundry knocks;
Been scorched with sun and wet with rain,
And soaked with snow, time and again.

Brave servitor! For Bunty's sake
You have held apples, sweets and cake,
Banana skins and chocolate bars,
And silkworms' eggs, and tadpole jars.

Now, your oft-girded strap has split;
Your faithful sides show many a slit;
With stains and creases here and there,
And ragged edges everywhere.

Your work is done! And by John's grace
She has a smart attaché case.
May this new comrade prove as true
And as long-suffering as you!

Fay Inchfawn

THE INN

WE take our pack, and jog our way again
    Towards the windy sunset and the night;
The inn is now behind us, out of sight,
Showing no welcome shine of window-pane,
But dark and silent standing by the way
As we go forward, seeing mile on mile
Sink out of sight—just for a little while
We rested, in the middle of the day.

Is there an end at last, and shall we reach,
By the faint glimmer of new-risen stars,
Our house at last, and find the heart-repose
Which is the ultimate desire of each
Poor traveller—ah, shall they drop the bars,
And the doors open? Dear my friend, who
      knows?

John Presland

THE USEFUL PLOUGH

A COUNTRY life is sweet;
   In moderate cold and heat,
To walk in the air, how pleasant and fair,
   In every field of wheat.
The fairest of flowers adorning the bowers,
   And every meadow's brow;
So that I say, no courtier may
Compare with them who clothe in grey,
   And follow the useful plough.

They rise with the morning lark,
   And labour till almost dark;
Then folding their sheep, they hasten to sleep;
   While every pleasant park
Next morning is ringing with birds that are singing
   On each green, tender bough.
With what content and merriment
Their days are spent, whose minds are bent
   To follow the useful plough!

Old song

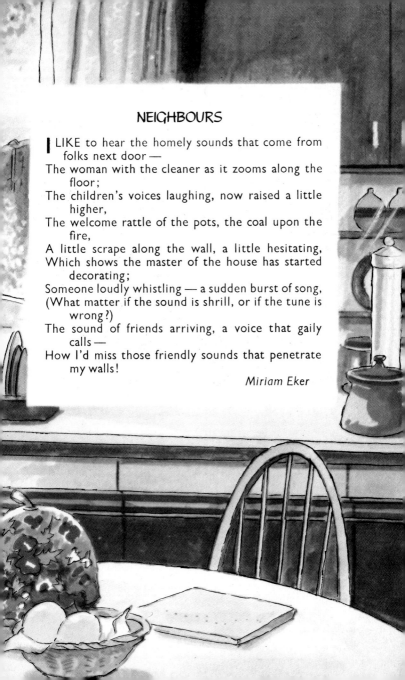

NEIGHBOURS

I LIKE to hear the homely sounds that come from
    folks next door —
The woman with the cleaner as it zooms along the
    floor;
The children's voices laughing, now raised a little
    higher,
The welcome rattle of the pots, the coal upon the
    fire,
A little scrape along the wall, a little hesitating,
Which shows the master of the house has started
    decorating;
Someone loudly whistling — a sudden burst of song,
(What matter if the sound is shrill, or if the tune is
    wrong?)
The sound of friends arriving, a voice that gaily
    calls —
How I'd miss those friendly sounds that penetrate
    my walls!

Miriam Eker

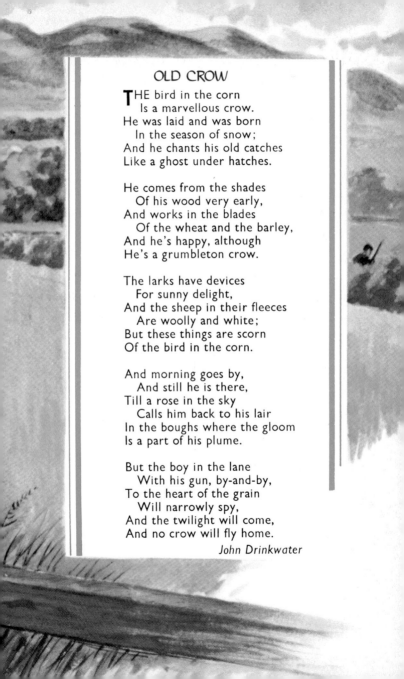

OLD CROW

THE bird in the corn
  Is a marvellous crow.
He was laid and was born
  In the season of snow;
And he chants his old catches
Like a ghost under hatches.

He comes from the shades
  Of his wood very early,
And works in the blades
  Of the wheat and the barley,
And he's happy, although
He's a grumbleton crow.

The larks have devices
  For sunny delight,
And the sheep in their fleeces
  Are woolly and white;
But these things are scorn
Of the bird in the corn.

And morning goes by,
  And still he is there,
Till a rose in the sky
  Calls him back to his lair
In the boughs where the gloom
Is a part of his plume.

But the boy in the lane
  With his gun, by-and-by,
To the heart of the grain
  Will narrowly spy,
And the twilight will come,
And no crow will fly home.

John Drinkwater

INSCRIPTION FOR AN OLD BED

THE wind's on the wold
  And the night is a-cold,
And Thames runs chill
'Twixt mead and hill.
But kind and dear
Is the old house here
And my heart is warm
'Midst winter's harm.
Rest then and rest,
And think of the best
'Twixt summer and spring,
When all birds sing
In the town of the tree,
And ye lie in me
And scarce dare move
Lest the earth and its love
Should fade away
Ere the full of the day.
I am old and have seen
Many things that have been:
Both grief and peace
And wane and increase.
No tale I tell
Of ill or well
But this I say:
Night treadeth on day,
And for worst or best
Right good is rest.

William Morris

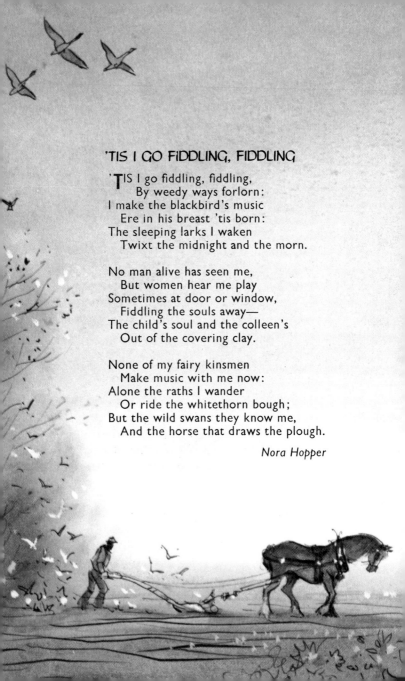

'TIS I GO FIDDLING, FIDDLING

'TIS I go fiddling, fiddling,
  By weedy ways forlorn:
I make the blackbird's music
  Ere in his breast 'tis born:
The sleeping larks I waken
  Twixt the midnight and the morn.

No man alive has seen me,
  But women hear me play
Sometimes at door or window,
  Fiddling the souls away—
The child's soul and the colleen's
  Out of the covering clay.

None of my fairy kinsmen
  Make music with me now:
Alone the raths I wander
  Or ride the whitethorn bough;
But the wild swans they know me,
  And the horse that draws the plough.

Nora Hopper

COTSWOLD HOLIDAY

IT is fun to wake up at the dawning,
   The cock's bugle crow ringing clear;
A scrabble of ducks in the garden,
    And cud-chewing cows edging near.

To stroll through the grass of a morning
    While others are slumbering still,
And watch the sun throw from its palette
    A roseate glow on the hill.

The hours are so dreary and drowsy,
    We savour the old ways at ease,
The unhurried pace of the country,
    The villages hid in the trees.

The manors, the farms and the churches
　　Seem out of the land to have grown,
With haze and with history mellowed,
　　And gold gleaming out of the stone.

Laburnum hangs lamps by the porches,
　　With hollyhocks regal and tall,
Soft fragrance of wallflower and roses,
　　And stillness and calm over all.

We find in the quiet seclusion,
　　From stresses and cares a release—
God surely bestowed on the Cotswolds
　　Abundance of favour and peace.

William Landles

WHEN THE WINDS BLOW

WHEN the winds blow,
   And the skies are shorn
Of the sun's bright light,
   And the bleak hills mourn,

When the rain sweeps
   Like an endless flood,
Drowning the leaves
   In the grieving wood,

When the night comes
   Like a long-drawn sigh,
And no star lights
   The dark of the sky,

Here, safe at home
   I shall not care
While the lamplight shines
   On your sun-bright hair!

Aileen E. Passmore

A BOY'S SONG

WITH lifted feet, hands still,
    I am poised, and down the hill
Dart, with heedful mind;
The air goes by in a wind.

Swifter and yet more swift,
Till the heart with a mighty lift
Makes the lungs laugh, the throat cry:—
" O bird, see; see, bird, I fly!

" Is this, is this your joy?
O bird, then I, though a boy,
For a golden moment share
Your feathery life in air! "

Say, heart, is there aught like this
In a world that is full of bliss?
'Tis more than skating, bound
Steel-shod to the level ground.

Speed slackens now, I float
Awhile in my airy boat;
Till, when the wheels scarce crawl,
My feet to the treadles fall.

Alas, that the longest hill
Must end in a vale, but still,
Who climbs with toil, wheresoe'er,
Shall find wings waiting there.

Henry Charles Beeching

TOMORROW

IN the downhill of life, when I find I'm declining,
   May my lot no less fortunate be
Than a snug elbow-chair can afford for reclining,
   And a cot that o'erlooks the wide sea;
With an ambling pad-pony to pace o'er the lawn,
   While I carol away idle sorrow,
And blithe as the lark that each day hails the dawn
   Look forward with hope for tomorrow.

With a porch at my door both for shelter and
      shade, too,
   As the sunshine or rain may prevail;
And a small spot of ground for the use of the
      spade, too,
   With a barn for the use of the flail;
A cow for my dairy, a dog for my game,
   And a purse when a friend wants to borrow—
I'll envy no nabob his riches or fame,
   Or what honours await him tomorrow.

And when I at last must throw off this frail cov'ring
   Which I've worn for threescore years and ten,
On the brink of the grave I'll not seek to keep
      hov'ring,
   Nor my thread wish to spin o'er again;
But my face in the glass I'll serenely survey,
   And with smiles count each wrinkle and furrow,
As this old worn-out stuff, which is threadbare
      today,
   May become everlasting tomorrow.

J. Collins

TO A BUTTERFLY

I'VE watched you now a full half-hour,
  Self-poised upon that yellow flower;
And, little Butterfly! indeed
I know not if you sleep or feed.
How motionless!—not frozen seas
More motionless! and then
What joy awaits you, when the breeze
Hath found you out among the trees,
And calls you forth again!

This plot of orchard ground is ours;
My trees they are, my sister's flowers;
Here rest your wings when they are weary;
Here lodge as in a sanctuary!
Come often to us, fear no wrong;
Sit near us on the bough!
We'll talk of sunshine and of song,
And summer days, when we were young;
Sweet childish days, that were as long
As twenty days are now.

                    William Wordsworth

HAD I A GOLDEN POUND

HAD I a golden pound to spend,
  My love should mend and sew no more;
And I would buy her a little quern,
  Easy to turn on the kitchen floor.

And for her windows curtains white,
  With birds in flight and flowers in bloom,
To face with pride the road to town
  And mellow down her sunlit room.

And with the silver change we'd prove
  The truth of Love to life's own end,
With hearts the years could but embolden,
  Had I a golden pound to spend.

Francis Ledwidge

TIME, YOU OLD GIPSY MAN

TIME, you old gipsy man,
  Will you not stay,
Put up your caravan
  Just for one day?

All things I'll give you
Will you be my guest,
Bells for your jennet
Of silver the best,
Goldsmiths shall beat you
A great golden ring,
Peacocks shall bow to you,
Little boys sing,
Oh, and sweet girls will
Festoon you with may,
Time, you old gipsy,
Why hasten away?

Last week in Babylon,
Last night in Rome,
Morning, and in the crush
Under Paul's dome;
Under Paul's dial
You tighten your rein—
Only a moment,
And off once again;
Off to some city
Now blind in the womb,
Off to another
Ere that's in the tomb.

Time, you old gipsy man,
  Will you not stay,
Put up your caravan
  Just for one day?

Ralph Hodgson

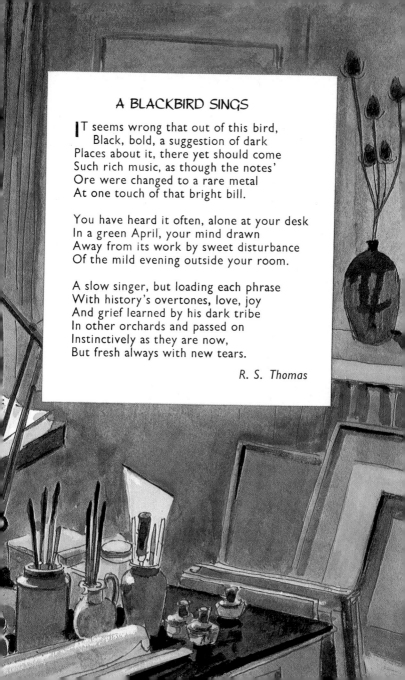

A BLACKBIRD SINGS

IT seems wrong that out of this bird,
   Black, bold, a suggestion of dark
Places about it, there yet should come
Such rich music, as though the notes'
Ore were changed to a rare metal
At one touch of that bright bill.

You have heard it often, alone at your desk
In a green April, your mind drawn
Away from its work by sweet disturbance
Of the mild evening outside your room.

A slow singer, but loading each phrase
With history's overtones, love, joy
And grief learned by his dark tribe
In other orchards and passed on
Instinctively as they are now,
But fresh always with new tears.

                                    R. S. Thomas

THE LOST CAT

SHE took a last and simple meal when there
were none to see her steal —
A jug of cream upon the shelf, a fish prepared
for dinner;
And now she walks a distant street with delicately
sandalled feet,
And no one gives her much to eat or weeps to
see her thinner.

O my beloved come again, come back in joy,
come back in pain,
To end our searching with a mew, or with a
purr our grieving;
And you shall have for lunch or tea whatever fish
swim in the sea
And all the cream that's meant for me — and
not a word of thieving!

E. V. Rieu

THE LAPFUL OF NUTS

WHENE'ER I see soft hazel eyes
 And nut-brown curls,
I think of those bright days I spent
 Among the Limerick girls;
When up through Cratla woods I went
 Nutting with thee,
And we pluck'd the glossy clustering fruit
 From many a bending tree.

Beneath the hazel boughs we sat,
 Thou, love, and I,
And the gather'd nuts lay in thy lap,
 Beneath thy downcast eye;
But little we thought of the store we'd won,
 I, love, or thou;
For our hearts were full, and we dared not own
 The love that's spoken now.

Oh, there's wars for willing hearts in Spain,
 And high Germanie!
And I'll come back, ere long, again
 With knightly fame and fee:
And I'll come back, if I ever come back,
 Faithful to thee,
That sat with thy white lap full of nuts,
 Beneath the hazel-tree.

Samuel Ferguson

THE VALLEY

A ROAD winds through the valley in a land I know
   afar,
And the hills rise up before it, robed in purple
   haze,
It is a road through twilight that seeks the evening
   star,
A road that I would journey as in remembered
   days.

The hills shut out the sunset, and golden are their
   brows,
And it is warm in the valley that slumbers at their
   feet,
When through the misty meadows they drive the
   lowing cows,
And the voices of the daytime die down the empty
   street.

The silence, like a curtain, falls on the sleeping
   hills,
Only the owl is wakeful, and the wind that wanders
   on;
And I can feel the silence, and my heart in exile
   fills
With yearning for the homeland, the days for ever
gone.

A road winds through the valley, it shines beneath
   the moon,
The hills rise black before it, the stars are bright
   above;
Oh, I would die tomorrow to gain my heart's one
   boon —
This night to see in moonlight the valley that I
   love!

Cecil Roberts

WASTED EFFORT

A GALAXY of blossoms
  Adorns my garden-bed;
In careless, gay abandon
  They multiply and spread
Till every nook and corner,
  A multi-coloured maze,
With golds and blues and crimsons
  Is riotously ablaze.

The dandelion and groundsel,
  The scarlet pimpernel,
The bright-eyed little daisies
  Are up (and doing well).
The small, determined chickweed
  Has shown her tiny face,
While thistles, sturdy, vigorous,
  Are flowering apace.

All grow luxuriant and lush
  With neither thought nor care,
*But where are those expensive seeds
  I bought and planted there?*

                    Gertrude Monro-Higgs

BELOW THE WEIR

BEYOND the punt the swallows go
    Like blue-black arrows to and fro,
Now stooping where the rushes grow,
    Now flashing o'er a shallow;
And overhead in blue and white
High Spring and Summer hold delight;
" All right!" the black-cap calls, " All right!"
    His mate says from the sallow.

I like to think, when I shall go
To this essential dust, that so
I yet may share in flowers that blow,
    And with such brave sights mingle,
If tossed by summer breeze on high
I'm carried where the cuckoos cry
And dropped beside old Thames to lie
    A sand-grain on a shingle.

Meanwhile the swallows flash and skim
Like blue-black arrows notched and trim,
And splendid kingcups lift a brim
    Of gold to king or peasant,
And 'neath a sky of blue and white
High Spring with Summer weaves delight:
" All right !" the black-cap calls, " All right!"
    And life is very pleasant.

Patrick R. Chalmers

THOMAS CLEGG

BEFORE I'll want
    Or starve, or beg,
I'd learn a trade
    Like Thomas Clegg.

For fifty years
    He's heel'd and soled,
For town and gown,
    Both young and old.

He sees us come
    And lets us go,
And knows us all
    From heel to toe.

He holds the nails
    Betwix his teeth,
Then pops them at
    The sole beneath.

Fixed in the last
    Athwart his lap,
Each nail receives
    But one shrewd tap.

Oh, I will want,
    Or starve, or beg,
Before I cobble
    Like Thomas Clegg!

A. C. Gordon Ross

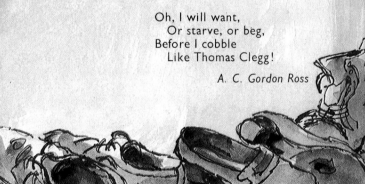

THERE IS A GARDEN

THERE is a garden in her face,
　Where roses and white lilies grow;
A heavenly paradise is that place,
　Wherein all pleasant fruits do flow.
There cherries grow which none can buy,
Till '' Cherry-ripe '' themselves do cry.

Those cherries fairly do enclose
　Of orient pearl a double row,
Which when her lovely laughter shows,
　They look like rosebuds filled with snow.
Yet them nor peer nor prince can buy,
Till '' Cherry-ripe '' themselves do cry.

Her eyes like angels watch them still,
　Her brows like bended bows do stand,
Threatening with piercing frowns to kill
　All that attempt with eye or hand
Those sacred cherries to come nigh,
Till '' Cherry-ripe '' themselves do cry.

Thomas Campion

SNOW

NO breath of wind,
   No gleam of sun —
Still the white snow
Whirls softly down —
Twig and bough
And blade and thorn
All in an icy
Quiet, forlorn.
Whispering, rustling,
Through the air,
On sill and stone,
Roof—everywhere,
It heaps its powdery
Crystal flakes,
Of every tree
A mountain makes;
Till pale and faint
At shut.of day,
Stoops from the West
One wintry ray.
And, feathered in fire,
Where ghosts the moon,
A robin shrills
His lonely tune.

Walter de la Mare

GRANDMOTHER'S GARDEN

OH, sweet were the roses the flower-girls were
   selling
  As slowly through London I journeyed today.
And, swiftly, a voice in my bosom was telling
   Of Grandmother's garden down Somerset way.

In a smoke-grimy lilac a thrush began singing,
   Think of it, think how the wallflowers are gay!
Think of the clematis round the porch clinging
   And you—only you—only you—are away!

By the low-lichened wall there are lilies tiptoeing,
   While columbines curtsy and butterflies stray,
And there's lad's love and larkspur and lavender
     growing
   In Grandmother's garden down Somerset way.

Then, round the next corner, a messenger met me,
   With whiffs of the lilac and scent of the may.
Ah, wind from the west, with what dreams you
     beset me
   Of Grandmother's garden down Somerset way.

Almost I can catch the faint chirp of the cricket,
   The croon of the doves as the twilight comes grey.
My nightingale sings in the little brown thicket
   And Grandmother waits in the dusk of the day.

Fay Inchfawn

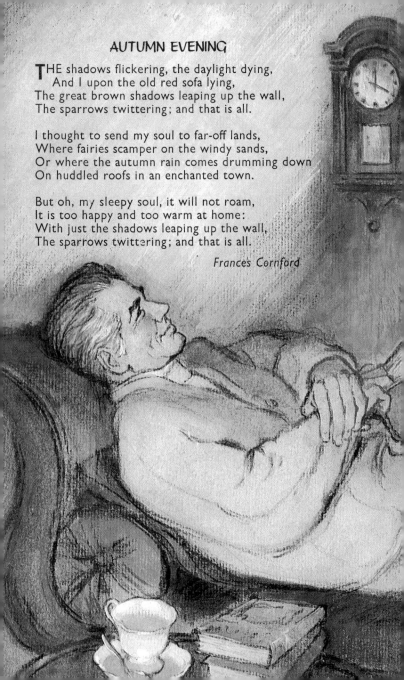

AUTUMN EVENING

THE shadows flickering, the daylight dying,
   And I upon the old red sofa lying,
The great brown shadows leaping up the wall,
The sparrows twittering; and that is all.

I thought to send my soul to far-off lands,
Where fairies scamper on the windy sands,
Or where the autumn rain comes drumming down
On huddled roofs in an enchanted town.

But oh, my sleepy soul, it will not roam,
It is too happy and too warm at home:
With just the shadows leaping up the wall,
The sparrows twittering; and that is all.

Frances Cornford

IN THE CATHEDRAL CLOSE

IN the Dean's porch a nest of clay
  With five small tenants may be seen,
Five solemn faces, each as wise
  As though its owner were a Dean;

Five downy fledglings in a row,
  Packed close, as in the antique pew
The school-girls are, whose foreheads clear
  At the *Venite* shine on you.

Day after day the swallows sit
  With scarce a stir, with scarce a sound,
But dreaming and digesting much
  They grow thus wise and soft and round.

They watch the Canons come to dine,
  And hear, the mullion-bars across,
Over the fragrant fruit and wine
  Deep talk of rood-screen and reredos.

. . . .

And somewhere 'mid yon Eastern suns,
    Under a white Greek architrave
At morn, or when the shaft of fire
    Lies large upon the Indian wave,

A sense of something dear gone-by
    Will stir, strange longings thrill the heart
For a small world embowered and close,
    Of which ye some time were a part.

Edward Dowden

LOVE ON THE MOUNTAIN

MY love comes down from the mountain
   Through the mists of dawn;
I look, and the star of the morning
   From the sky is gone.

My love comes down from the mountain,
   At dawn, dewy-sweet;
Did you step from the star to the mountain,
   O little white feet?

O whence came your twining tresses
   And your shining eyes,
But out of the gold of the morning
   And the blue of the skies?

The misty mountain is burning
   In the sun's red fire,
And the heart in my breast is burning
   And lost in desire.

I follow you into the valley
   But no word can I say;
To the East or the West I will follow
   Till the dusk of my day.

Thomas Boyd

THE PATCHWORK QUILT

THE gnarled fingers smooth the silk
  Of orange, gold, and green, and milk;
The oyster satin and brocade
Hold memories that will not fade.

The muslin worn at her first ball
In that sweet time beyond recall,
Lies captured by a silken thread,
Hard by a square of deepest red.

And stitched against the peach and brown,
Rest gleaming fragments of the gown
She wore with pride one morn in May —
That golden time — her wedding day.

The pieces many stories tell
To her who knew their touch so well,
Whose gnarled old fingers smooth the silk
Of orange, gold, and green, and milk.

Violet Hall

PACK, CLOUDS, AWAY

PACK, clouds, away, and welcome day,
  With night we banish sorrow;
Sweet air blow soft, mount larks aloft
  To give my Love good-morrow!
Wings from the wind to please her mind
  Notes from the lark I'll borrow;
Bird, prune thy wing, nightingale sing,
  To give my Love good-morrow;
    To give my Love good-morrow
    Notes from them both I'll borrow.

Wake from thy nest, robin-redbreast,
  Sing, birds, in every furrow;
And from each hill, let music shrill
  Give my fair Love good-morrow!
Blackbird and thrush in every bush,
  Stare, linnet, and cock-sparrow!
You pretty elves, amongst yourselves
  Sing my fair Love good-morrow;
    To give my Love good-morrow
    Sing, birds, in every furrow!

Thomas Heywood

AFTER SUMMER HOLIDAYS

THE best part of holidays
    Is the coming home,
Happy feet are they that turn
    From the world to roam.
Just the first small glimpse you get
    Seems to thrill you through,
Of your house among the trees
    Smiling out at you.

Coming home to plants and things
    On the window-sill.
(Same old row of poplar trees
    There against the hill).
Rooms look kind of cosy-like
    At the dusk of day,
Seem to think more of the place
    Since we've been away.

Coming home to school and work,
    (Dear old routine things);
Health in every pulsing vein,
    Seem to move on wings.
Dear familiar rooms and beds,
    Fireplace and den,
Holidays are wonderful
    — When you're home again!

Edna Jaques

THE CITY CLERK

'TIS strange how my head runs on! 'tis a puzzle
    to understand
Such fancies stirring in me, for a whiff of hay in the
    Strand!

I see the old farmhouse, and garden wall, and the
    bees;
I see the mowers stretch'd, with their bottles, under
    the trees;

I hear the little brook a-ripple down in the dell;
I hear the old-folk croon—'' Our son, he is doing
    well!''

O yes, I am doing well; but I'd be again, for a day,
A simple farmer's lad, among the girls in the hay.

Thomas Ashe

A RENDEZVOUS WITH SPRING

COMING quickly — coming quickly — coming
    quickly — sings the train,
      Sings the train upon a Friday afternoon;
Our wheels are rolling westwards; we shall soon
      be home again;
      We shall rendezvous with spring, quite soon.
There's Risborough behind us, there's Bicester
      now in sight;
      Then it's Ardley, and it's Aynho, and we're
        through;
We shall sleep among the wild things, and beneath
      the stars tonight,
      At our springtide rendezvous.

Tomorrow we shall wander where the crooning
      pigeons nest,
      Where the moss is starry underneath the
        trees;
We shall bare our heads in welcome to a wind
      that's from the west,
      A wind that stirs the first anemones.
There'll be life, in all its promise, in every
      woodland ride
      And above, there'll be a sky that's white and
        blue,
And somewhere there'll be daffodils that lift their
      heads in pride
      At our springtime rendezvous.

Hubert Phillips

HOUSE ON A HILL

A LITTLE house on a windy hill
   And, beyond, a starry sky,
Sleeping fields in the moonlight chill
   And the keen wind raging high;
But secure, within, a home of peace
   Warm and locked from the night,
Music and generous talk and ease
   In the soft, dim candle-light.

For a golden voice with the 'cello rose,
   Two hands touched ivory keys,
And our hearts were lulled to soft repose
   With love-lorn melodies;
And the lonely wind like a spirit went
   Wailing along the night,
Heard in the pause when the music, spent,
   Died in a faint delight.

Ah, the laurels of years and the triumphs of years
   Shall fade, but the little things
Will all come back with a grace of tears
   On soft, inaudible wings,
And the wind shall wail o'er a phantom hill,
   The music come to an end,
And one will mourn the voice grown still,
   The eyes of a vanished friend.

Cecil Roberts

EVEN THEN...

SUPPOSE the very things I hate
    Should all come trooping to my gate;
Suppose my currant jam won't set,
Suppose my washing day is wet,
And then suppose the clothes-line breaks
Just as the littlest one awakes.

Suppose the butcher sends me meat
That no one in the house can eat;
Or Mrs Char, who doesn't think,
Lets half a lemon down the sink;
Or queer relations come to stay
Just when John has to be away.

Well, even then
There still will be
God, and the universe—
And me!

Fay Inchfawn

OAK TREES

OAK trees, how stately do they grow,
    Like old dowagers in a row,
They have a pride, too, I declare,
You'd almost think they were aware
Of their importance, if you please,
Their prestige in the world of trees.

Whene'er I see a spreading oak
I think of common sturdy folk,
Of an old room with a beamed ceiling
And corner cupboards just revealing
Blue plates and platters standing up
And the pale half-moon of a cup.

I think of ships ghost-white with foam
Headed down the long seas for home,
Their oaken beams and creaking sides
Straining against the wind and tides,
Clean-breasted as a bird in flight
Cleaving the frosty air of night.

I think of Druid priests of old,
Of all the ancient stories told
Of knights in armour, ladies fair,
Of little cottages . . . clean air,
Where oak trees spread their branches
    wide
And grow in majesty and pride.

Edna Jaques

TWILIGHT ON TWEED

THREE crests against the saffron sky,
  Beyond the purple plain,
The kind remember'd melody
  Of Tweed once more again.

Wan water from the Border hills,
  Dear voice from the old years,
Thy distant music lulls and stills,
  And moves to quiet tears.

Like a loved ghost thy fabled flood
  Fleets through the dusky land;
Where Scott, come home to die, has stood,
  My feet returning stand.

A mist of memory broods and floats,
  The Border waters flow;
The air is full of ballad notes
  Borne out of long ago.

Old songs that sung themselves to me,
  Sweet through a boy's day-dream,
While trout below the blossom'd tree
  Flash'd in the golden stream.

Twilight, and Tweed, and Eildon Hill,
  Fair and too fair you be;
You tell me that the voice is still
  That should have welcomed me.

Andrew Lang

THE CHILD AND THE PAINT-BOX

OUTSIDE my window I can see
    Frozen pond and naked tree;
The birds look big and black, with wings
Puffed out to keep them warm, poor things;
The paths are neatly swept of snow
That I may walk there, to and fro.
But I shall stay indoors instead
And paint these pictures blue and red,
Burnt sienna and Vandyke brown,
Crimson lake for the lady's gown;
The King is yellow beside the Queen
In flounces of beautiful ultramarine.
I'll paint the prince and the courtiers, too
With lots of scarlet and Prussian blue,
With jewels and peacocks as bright as you please,
And oranges growing on all the trees.

Eiluned Lewis

THE FALL

FLYING leaves, sighing leaves,
 Bustling and rustling leaves,
Dead leaves and red leaves, russet and brown:
 Tattered and scattered leaves,
 Trodden and sodden leaves —
Leaves of October are all falling down.

 Dancing leaves, prancing leaves,
 Old leaves and gold leaves,
Gay leaves and bay leaves blown through the
        town:
 Rolling leaves, strolling leaves,
 Laughing and daffing leaves —
Now in October they're all falling down.

 Little leaves, brittle leaves,
 Dying and drying leaves,
Falling and calling, they clutch Autumn's gown.
 Aspen leaves quivering,
 Willow leaves shivering —
Leaves of October are all falling down.

                                    Agnes Hall

ARABELLA AND SALLY ANN

ARABELLA was a schoolgirl,
  So was Sally Ann.
Hasty pudding can't be thicker
  Than two schoolgirls can.

These were thick as schoolgirls can be,
  Deathless love they swore,
Vowed that naught on earth should part them—
  One forever more.

They grew up as schoolgirls will do,
  Went to parties, too,
And as oft before has happened,
  Suitors came to woo.

But as fate or luck would have it,
  One misguided man
Favoured blue-eyed Arabella
  More than Sally Ann.

And, of course, it made no difference
  That the laws are such
That he could not wed two women,
  Though they wished it much.

So a coolness rose between them,
    And the cause—a man.
Cold was Arabella—very;
    Colder Sally Ann.

Now they call each other " creature ",
    What is still more sad—
Bella, though she won the treasure,
    Wishes Sally had.

Paul Carson

A THANKSGIVING TO GOD

LORD, Thou hast given me a cell
    Wherein to dwell;
A little house, whose humble roof
    Is weatherproof;
Under the spars of which I lie
    Both soft and dry.
Where Thou, my chamber for to ward,
    Hast set a guard
Of harmless thoughts, to watch and keep
    Me while I sleep.
Low is my porch, as is my fate,
    Both void of state;
And yet the threshold of my door
    Is worn by the poor,
Who hither come, and freely get
    Good words or meat.
Like as my parlour, so my hall,
    And kitchen small;
A little buttery, and therein
    A little bin,
Which keeps my little loaf of bread
    Unchipt, unflead.
Some brittle sticks of thorn or brier
    Make me a fire,
Close by whose living coal I sit,
    And glow like it.

Robert Herrick

SONG OF AN ANCIENT HEDGER

I'M slow, they say,
  In body and soul,
I live in a lone,
  Forsaken hole.

I know the lore
  Of brooks and ponds,
Of thorns and briars,
  And withy-wands.

And I have friends
  Of feather and fur,
One brown mouse, and
  A kingfisher.

And many a venturous
  Foal would stray,
And many a lamb
  Would lose its way,

And many a yearling
  Would be gone,
If it were not
  For Hedger John.

Some folks will nod,
  And some just stare
And never see me—
  Still, I'm there;

And in Spring dusk,
  Or Winter gloam,
I have a star
  To light me home.

Fay Inchfawn

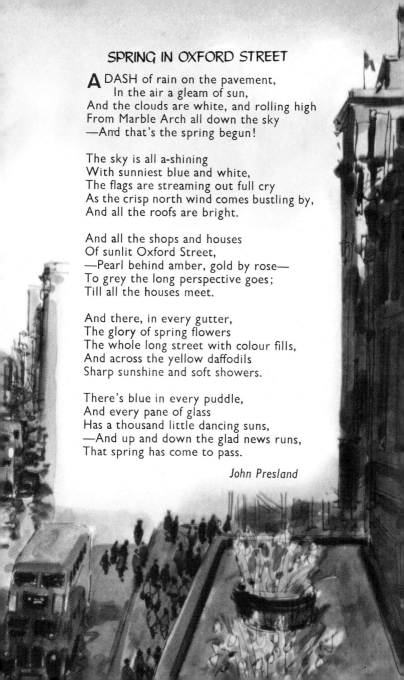

SPRING IN OXFORD STREET

A DASH of rain on the pavement,
  In the air a gleam of sun,
And the clouds are white, and rolling high
From Marble Arch all down the sky
—And that's the spring begun!

The sky is all a-shining
With sunniest blue and white,
The flags are streaming out full cry
As the crisp north wind comes bustling by,
And all the roofs are bright.

And all the shops and houses
Of sunlit Oxford Street,
—Pearl behind amber, gold by rose—
To grey the long perspective goes;
Till all the houses meet.

And there, in every gutter,
The glory of spring flowers
The whole long street with colour fills,
And across the yellow daffodils
Sharp sunshine and soft showers.

There's blue in every puddle,
And every pane of glass
Has a thousand little dancing suns,
—And up and down the glad news runs,
That spring has come to pass.

John Presland

I LOVE MY LOVE

DO you ask what the birds say? The sparrow,
    the dove,
The linnet and thrush say, " I love, and I love!"
In the winter they're silent, the wind is so strong ;
What it says I don't know, but it sings a loud song.
But green leaves and blossoms, and sunny warm
    weather,
And singing and loving—all come back together.
The lark is so brimful of gladness and love,
The green fields below him, the blue sky above,
That he sings, and he sings, and forever sings he,
" I love my Love and my Love loves me."

S. T. Coleridge

ACKNOWLEDGMENTS

Our thanks to Violet Hall for "The Market Square" and "The Patchwork Quilt"; to the Society of Authors and Miss Eiluned Lewis for "The Child And The Paint-Box" and "To Miranda In A Donkey-Cart"; to Gertrude Monro-Higgs for "Head-Gear" and "Wasted Effort"; to Miriam Eker for "Neighbours"; to Richard Rieu for "The Lost Cat" by E. V. Rieu; to A. C. Gordon Ross for "Thomas Clegg"; to the Literary Trustees of Walter de la Mare and the Society of Authors for "Snow"; to Francis Cornford and W. H. Allen Ltd. for "Autumn Evening" from *For Your Delight;* to Edna Jaques for "After Summer Holidays" and "Oak Trees"; to William Landles for "Cotswold Holiday"; to Charles Griffiths for "When The Winds Blow" by Aileen E. Passmore; to Methuen & Co. Ltd. for "Some Wishes" and "Below The Weir" from *A Peck O' Maut*; to Sidgwick & Jackson Ltd. for "Old Crow"; to Eleanor Farjeon and Michael Joseph for "The Carol Singers" from *Silver Sand and Snow*; to Ward Lock Ltd. for "Grandmother's Garden", "Even Then" and "Song of An Ancient Hedger" by Fay Inchfawn.